SAVAGE IN LIMBO

A CONCERT PLAY
BY JOHN PATRICK SHANLEY

★

DRAMATISTS
PLAY SERVICE
INC.

SAVAGE IN LIMBO
Copyright © 1986, John Patrick Shanley

All Rights Reserved

SPECIAL NOTE

SAVAGE IN LIMBO was originally presented as a staged reading at the 1984 National Playwrights Conference at the Eugene O'Neill Memorial Theatre Center. In September 1985, it was produced by the Double Image Theatre (Max D. Mayer, Artistic Director; Leslie Urdang, Managing Director) in New York City, where it was directed by Mark Linn-Baker; the sets were by Adrianne Lobel; the costumes were by Debra Tennenbaum; the lights were by Stephen Strawbridge; the production stage managers were Ruth Kreshka and William H. Lang. The cast, in order of appearance, was as follows:

MURK .... Randle Mell
APRIL WHITE............................ Jayne Haynes
DENISE SAVAGE .... Deborah Hedwall
LINDA ROTUNDA.................... Mary McDonnell
TONY ARONICA .... Larry Joshua

AUTHOR'S NOTE

In a concert play the audience, at least in my mind, is included in the world which the characters inhabit. And the play itself is more a series of related emotional and intellectual events than a conventional story. The characters are given more room, *more stage*, to express themselves than the restraints of naturalism would allow. And I hope of course, too, that there is a certain musical performance quality to it all.

This play is dedicated to all those good assassins
who contributed to the death of my former self.

4

CAST OF CHARACTERS

MURK. A big man, red-haired and baby-faced. He has no sense of humor. He does not pour drinks; he produces them from nowhere. He has a wooden foot.

APRIL WHITE. A beat-up, tired, vulnerable woman with beautiful, damaged eyes. She can go from serenity to hysteria without showing a seam.

DENISE SAVAGE. She's small, wild-haired, strong, belligerent, determined, dissatisfied, and scared. She is in pain, paranoid, and full of hunger. She has hungry ears.

LINDA ROTUNDA. A done-up, attractive, overripe Italian woman. She pronounces the name Anthony as "Antony," and the word virgin as "version." She is physically very womanly and very strong.

TONY ARONICA. A streamlined Italian stud with a streak of self-doubt and a yearning sweetness.

All of the characters are thirty-two years old.

The play is informed by the occasional paranoid silence.

All characters enter through the audience.

SAVAGE IN LIMBO

*The interior of Scales, a Bronx bar. Two dead plants provide
the only decoration. There are no bottles visible. There are no
mirrors. Downstage, a goodly distance apart, are two small
rectangular tables. One chair per table. The bar is unclean, the
tables vaguely dirty, the air stale.*

*The floor, which is shaped like a trapezoid with the narrow
end Upstage, is green and white linoleum that's coming up in
places. There's a blackened rectangular mark, Down Right,
where a jukebox used to be. The floor has about it a live performance feel, for the concert which is about to take place.*

*The place is lit too, too brightly, a powerful incandescent light
which permits no lies.*

*From the opening of the house, Murk and April are onstage.
When Murk is in his usual state, he is still. He's wearing a
presentable shirt and tie, khaki trousers and a web belt, and
black oxford workshoes. He's regarding April. April is sitting
on the only stool, at the end of the bar, Left. She's sleeping, her
head resting in her arms. Murk decides to wake her.*

MURK. April. April. April. April.

APRIL. What?

MURK. You were asleep.

APRIL. On the bar?

MURK. Yeah.

APRIL. No.

MURK. Yeah, you were.

APRIL. Okay if you say so. Top me off, Murk. I'm losing my
head.

MURK. Where's your money?

APRIL. I don't got no money.

MURK. You got no money, I don't serve you. (*He serves her a
shot, in a delicate little glass. She sips it. Enter Denise Savage. She stomps*

in and looks around. She's dissatisfied with all she sees. She's wearing a rather limp navy blue dress and black pumps. She carries a black bag, not too big, that she seems to want to throw, but she doesn't know what to throw it at.)

SAVAGE. What time is it?

MURK. Seven-thirty.

SAVAGE. Where is everybody? Where is somebody? Where is any fuckin body?

MURK. It's Monday night.

SAVAGE. I wanna have a good time.

MURK. Come on, Savage. It's Monday night.

SAVAGE. As if that made a difference. Why don't you put some fuckin nuts on the bar for Chrissake?

MURK. We don't have any nuts.

SAVAGE. Then somethin. Cheese doodles. Make a fuckin attempt.

MURK. You hungry?

SAVAGE. No.

MURK. Why don't you sit down?

SAVAGE. I don't wanna.

MURK. Alright. Stand up.

SAVAGE. I've got energy. Do you understand what I'm saying? I'm young. I'm strong. I just ate two Cornish game hens and a buncha broccoli. It's only seven-thirty. I don't feel like watching television once more for the rest of my life and I can't sit in that apartment that smells like a catbox with my mother who looks like a dead walrus for one more second or I will die. I will. So I put on a dress and my black pumps and I got lotsa cash and here I am. What's happening?

MURK. Why don't you try Cotter's?

SAVAGE. Cotter's is dead.

MURK. Then the P.C.?

SAVAGE. The P.C. is totally beat.

MURK. So sit down. It's Monday night all over.

SAVAGE. Wait a minute. Oh no, man. Don't tell me this. Where's the jukebox?

MURK. It broke. It started to smell like burning, and they took it out. We'll get another one in a couple of days.

SAVAGE. No jukebox?

MURK. Not tonight.

8

SAVAGE. I gotta feeling like something's chasing me.

MURK. That's not my problem.

SAVAGE. I gotta feeling like the house is on fire.

MURK. Uh-huh. (*Overwhelmed, Savage goes to the* D.L. *table and sits. She takes a worn pack of cards from her bag, and starts setting up for solitaire.*) What are you drinking?

SAVAGE. Nothing.

MURK. You gotta have something.

SAVAGE. Why?

MURK. Rules.

SAVAGE. White wine.

MURK. Alright. It's a dollar. I ain't serving you over there, and you gotta pay as you go.

SAVAGE. Why?

MURK. Rules.

SAVAGE. Alright. (*She goes, pays, takes wine back to her table.*) Murk?

MURK. What?

SAVAGE. You wanna shoot a game of pool?

MURK. No. (*Murk produces a watering can and comes out from behind the bar. He limps. He waters the two plants.*)

SAVAGE. Murk, why you water those plants? They're dead.

MURK. They don't know that. (*Enter Linda Rotunda, a done-up, attractive, overripe Italian girl. She comes in, sits down, and starts crying.*) What are you having?

SAVAGE. Hey. Are you blind? Give her a minute.

MURK. Alright.

SAVAGE. Linda?

LINDA. Denise?

SAVAGE. Hi.

LINDA. Hi.

SAVAGE. Do you want me not to notice that you're crying?

LINDA. I don't care who knows.

MURK. What are you having?

LINDA. A rusty nail. No ice.

MURK. Alright.

LINDA. I gotta situation here, but I don't know you good enough to talk about this.

SAVAGE. Comon. We went to school together.

LINDA. Grammar school only.

9

SAVAGE. So we're not friends. Cry by yourself.

LINDA. No. Hey. I can't go home. It's too early. My mother would know something is wrong. She'd be in my face inna minute.

SAVAGE. You wanna shoot a game of pool?

LINDA. No.

MURK. Your drink's here. Two dollars.

LINDA. Oh.

SAVAGE. Let it sit up there a minute. It drives him crazy. Why you crying?

LINDA. It's my boyfriend Anthony. Something's gone wrong with him.

SAVAGE. That's Tony Aronica, right?

LINDA. Yeah.

SAVAGE. The one who wears leather pants.

LINDA. Sometimes he does.

SAVAGE. Incredibly good-looking.

LINDA. Yeah, that's him.

SAVAGE. He knocked you up last year.

LINDA. Where'd you hear that?

SAVAGE. I heard it.

LINDA. Nobody knocked me up.

SAVAGE. Now that's pushin it, Linda. You're a neighborhood joke. You get knocked up every time you stop walking. It's stupid to lie about it. Everybody knows. You're sloppy and you're fertile.

LINDA. Are you bein nasty to me?

SAVAGE. No. That's the way I am. Comes a bein lonely. That's why I never hadda a boyfriend like Tony Aronica. At least that's one a the reasons.

MURK. Hey. Pick up your drink.

SAVAGE. See? It drives him nuts. It preys on his mind. Let him wait.

MURK. You can leave it here all night for what I care. But it's pay-as you-go. Two dollars. I'm waiting. (*Linda goes, pays, takes drink back to table.*)

SAVAGE. He's never grown up. He still thinks he's playin Simon Says in the playground.

MURK. I never played Simon Says.

SAVAGE. Well, whatever.

10

MURK. I played War.

SAVAGE. Bang, bang.

MURK. Shut up, Savage.

SAVAGE. You can't take no back and forth at all, can you?

MURK. I said shut up.

SAVAGE. Okay, don't get shook up. (*To Linda.*) So, what's wrong with you? What's the story? Did you get knocked up again?

LINDA. No. It's Anthony. He's gone crazy.

SAVAGE. Is he hittin you?

LINDA. No.

SAVAGE. What's he doin?

LINDA. He wants to see other women.

SAVAGE. What?

LINDA. He wants to see other women.

SAVAGE. And for this you think he's crazy, huh? You are a pisser.

LINDA. You don't understand.

SAVAGE. I understand that. That's very common.

LINDA. No, no. You don't understand.

SAVAGE. Have it your own way.

LINDA. He wants to see ugly women.

SAVAGE. They may look that way to you, honey, but I guess he sees 'em different.

LINDA. You don't understand. He told me. He says, Linda, I wanna see ugly girls.

SAVAGE. He said that?

LINDA. Yes.

SAVAGE. Well, what did he mean?

LINDA. He meant what he said.

SAVAGE. But that's not possible. Men don't go after women they think are ugly. If they end up with an ugly woman, it's because they made a mistake and they think she's good-lookin. Alright a drunk, a crazy guy, or a loser. But a guy like Tony? A guy like Tony Aronica would never end up with an ugly woman. You know why? He's just got too much dog in 'em. He thinks like a dog.

LINDA. What are you tellin me? You're tellin me nothin. I tell you what's goin on, and you tell me it ain't goin on. It's goin on. Anthony wants to see ugly girls cause I don't know why, but

11

that's the fuckin news and don't tell me otherwise. Every Monday night I go to his place and we spend time together, and this night I go and he's got this look in his eye. Like he knows somethin, and like he never seen me before. I got a scared feelin right away. I touch him but he puts my hand away. He says he wants to talk. What's he wanna talk about before we go to bed? What's there to talk about? When a woman wants to talk to a man, it's cause she wants the man to see her better. When it's the other way, when the man stops you from touchin to talk, what's there to talk about? It's gotta be bad. I tried to keep him from talkin. I turned myself on. But there was somethin in his mind. Even my mother sees what Anthony's got. Even my mother. She'd like a taste. She knows where I'm goin on Monday nights. I don't come home till late, the mornin sometimes, but she don't say anything. Any other time she would. But she knows where I go, and she wants it for me. Once I was goin, and she whispered to me so's my father wouldn't hear, Take it, Linda. That's all. Take it, Linda. And I did. And now he don't wanna see me cause he wants to see ugly women. I said I'd be ugly for him, but he said no. It didn't work that way. I'm so ashamed. I feel ugly. I feel fat. Anthony don't want me no more.

SAVAGE. You're not fat. You're almost fat. But you're not fat. You wanna play some cards?

LINDA. No.

SAVAGE. These cards are disgusting anyway. I left 'em near the humidifier one night and they got all spongy. I got the humidifier cause my mother was dryin out. She never goes anywhere, she can't, and we got so much heat in that fuckin apartment — I looked at her one day and she looked like a dead plant. So I went out and I got the humidifier and I run it every night. She still looks like freeze-dried shit, but I feel better cause I did somethin. I didn't just take it. I didn't just fuckin accept it. I believe in action. Anyway, between the humidity and my sloppy ways, these cards are real crappy. Some of these Sister Rosita's, you know, these witchtellers, they're supposed to be able to see your future inna pack a cards. I look at these cards, I never see anything about my future. I just see my fuckin life. I'm gonna go insane.

LINDA. What are you talkin about?

SAVAGE. I'm talkin about tension. I'm talkin about somethin

12

snappin at your heels, but you can't get away. Bein apart from everybody else. Bein alone. There's a wall there. Like you're inna glass box, a bee inna jar, dreamin about flowers, smellin your own . . . death. People look at you, it's through somethin. You touch somebody, there's somethin over your hand.

LINDA. I don't get you.

SAVAGE. I'm tryin to tell you somethin, but it's not easy.

LINDA. So tell me anyway.

SAVAGE. I'm a virgin.

LINDA. What?

SAVAGE. You heard me. You're just astounded. I'm a virgin.

LINDA. Why you tellin me a lie?

SAVAGE. In the beginnin, it was just bad luck. I'm not like you, and I got a big mouth, and well, it's easy not to lose it at first. You're scared, they're scared, somebody says: Boo, and everybody runs away. At least that's the way it was for me. To start with. But then it became a thing. Most everybody I knew lost it, you know, over a certain period a time, and there I was, still in the wrapper. It woulda been easy to lose it then. But it became a thing, you know? I felt different. I felt like I was holdin out for somethin. Not some guy, not just some guy. I felt like I was holdin out for somethin, sayin no, no, I'm not takin that life just cause it was the first one I was offered. So here I am. I'm thirty-two. And I'm still sayin no, no. And I still only got offered the one life, and I still don't want that one.

LINDA. You're a virgin?

SAVAGE. Yeah.

LINDA. Wow.

SAVAGE. Say somethin.

LINDA. What's it like?

SAVAGE. It's like holdin your breath, only you never have to let go. No, that's not what it's like . . .

LINDA. I never knew anybody grown up who never, you know . . . I feel like you know somethin I don't know.

SAVAGE. Well, I know you know somethin I don't know.

LINDA. Yeah, but everybody I know knows what I know. Except you. It's like common knowledge. But what you know, it's like a secret. How does it feel?

SAVAGE. I feel strong. Like I'm wearin chains and I could snap 'em any time. I feel ready. I go to work and I feel like I

13

could take over the company, but I just type. I go home and I see my mother in her chair and I feel like I could pick her up with one hand and chuck her out the window and roll up the rug and throw a big party. Everybody's invited. I go to the library and I wanna take the books down off the shelves and open all the books on the tables and argue with everybody about ideas. I wanna think out loud. I wanna think out loud with other people. You know what's wrong with everybody? Too smart. I know it sounds crazy. I know. But it's true. Everybody's too smart. It's like everybody knows everything and everybody argued everything and everything got hashed out and settled the day before I was born. It's not fair. They know about gravity so nobody talks about gravity. It's a dead issue. Look at me. My feet are stuck to the fuckin floor. Fantastic. But no. That's gravity. Forget it. It's been done it's been said it's been thought, so fuck it. It's not fair. I've been shut outta everything that mighta been good by a smartness around that won't let me think not one new thing. And it's been like that with love, too. You're a little girl and you see the movies and maybe you talk to your mother and you definitely talk to your friends and then you know, right? So you go ahead and you do love. And somethin a what somebody told ya inna movie or in your ear is what love is. And where the fuck are you then, that's what I wanna know? Where the fuck are you when you've done love, and you can point to love, and you can name it, and love is the same as gravity the same as everything else, and everything else is a totally dead fuckin issue?
LINDA. That's what it's like to be a virgin?
SAVAGE. That's part of it. Maybe that's the good part.
LINDA. You wanna be my friend?
SAVAGE. I don't know how.
LINDA. Me neither.
SAVAGE. Why you want me?
LINDA. Cause I gotta make a change, and you're different.
SAVAGE. What are you gonna do?
LINDA. Things have got to where I got to make a change.
MURK. Hey, keep it down.
SAVAGE. Back off.
LINDA. All I had was Monday. I just marked time till Monday. I ain't got Monday no more so I gotta make a change. Everything's doin shit on me an changin on me an lookin different than

14

it was before and now there ain't no Monday and I'm thirty-two and my mother's gonna be on my case again my sucky life and I'll be fucking guys under staircases and I gotta make a change for myself this time no matter how much it hurts, I don't want to, scared, or it's goodbye Linda for sure. You gotta help me.

SAVAGE. How?

LINDA. Don't ask me that. That's the question. I don't know. But I gotta change.

SAVAGE. I gotta ask cause so do I, too.

LINDA. What are we gonna do?

SAVAGE. I don't know.

LINDA. I'm scared. I feel so scared.

SAVAGE. Why?

LINDA. I gotta move outta my whole house.

SAVAGE. So move.

LINDA. Why ain't you moved outta your house? (*No answer.*) Why ain't you moved outta your house?

SAVAGE. I can't do that.

LINDA. Why not?

SAVAGE. My mother's a shut-in. She's trapped. I can't leave her.

LINDA. Ain't we shut-in's, too?

SAVAGE. I gotta good room. I got books there that I read. And I gotta refill the humidifier all the time. My mother, she can only walk on canes. I figured it out. Without me, she'd die in three days.

LINDA. You're scared, too.

SAVAGE. No, I'm not.

LINDA. Yeah, you are.

SAVAGE. Yeah.

LINDA. I thought you weren't.

SAVAGE. I'm scared of everything. I see what could go wrong with everything so I don't do nothin. I got this one thing in me that I hate. I'm a coward.

LINDA. We gotta be friends.

SAVAGE. Alright.

LINDA. I ain't never been friends with a girl. I guess this is it.

SAVAGE. I ain't never been friends with nobody. I ain't had the time. I got my mother. I got the job. I just talk at people, which is lonely. I honestly could just fall down from loneliness.

15

LINDA. Maybe . . . Maybe we should do somethin together.

SAVAGE. For instance what?

LINDA. I don't know. Maybe we should go dancin together or somethin.

SAVAGE. Dancin?

LINDA. Somethin.

SAVAGE. I don't dance.

LINDA. Somethin.

SAVAGE. Maybe we should, I don't know, getta apartment. Together.

LINDA. Yeah? That'd be a step out, wouldn't it?

SAVAGE. It's an idea.

LINDA. So we're like girlfriends now, right? We're girlfriends, talkin to each other about bein roommates.

APRIL. Who wants a friend? I'll be somebody's friend.

MURK. Be quiet.

APRIL. No. I mean it. I'll be friends with anybody who wants to be friends.

MURK. Go to sleep.

APRIL. I can't go to sleep, Murk, even though I'm real tired. If I go to sleep, you'll throw me out. That's the rules and that's justice. Who wants a friend? Do I know you?

SAVAGE. Sure you know us. We all went to Saint Anthony's together.

APRIL. Okay, Saint Anthony's. What's your name?

SAVAGE. Denise Savage.

APRIL. And you?

LINDA. Linda Rotunda.

APRIL. And what's my name?

LINDA. I don't remember her.

SAVAGE. Your name is April. April White.

APRIL. That's right.

LINDA. You're April White?

APRIL. That's right.

LINDA. Oh my God.

APRIL. Pretty bad, huh?

LINDA. You look different.

APRIL. Pretty bad.

MURK. You look outstanding.

APRIL. Thanks.

16

LINDA. You re April White. I'm sorry. I didn't mean to . . . You were supposed to be a nun.

APRIL. Was I? Oops.

LINDA. You were supposed to become a nun, and work with sick people in India. You made a little speech in front of the class. About becoming a Maryknoll nun. You shook. I thought you were beautiful.

APRIL. I was.

SAVAGE. Yeah, she was.

MURK. She is still.

APRIL. You got pregnant. I remember. You disappeared in the middle of the eighth. Sister Theresa said you'd swallowed a pin. Then the girls started whispering. I didn't like that. That whispering number. It was slimey. It was a slimey way to act. But I remember. You got pregnant.

LINDA. You got a big mouth.

APRIL. Sorry. I was just placing you.

MURK. Here. Take a drink.

APRIL. What? Is the haze goin off me? Murk keeps me inna special haze and I keep him company. I didn't become a nun causa Father Rogan. Father Rogan was this priest he was cute he had premature grey hair and he useta tell me about becomin a nun in India. But then one day in the Sixties he got tired a bein a premature grey priest he quit. But he stayed in the neighborhood. He went out he stood onna streetcorner in civilian clothes and hung out. He got fat he liked to drink beer quart bottles of beer. He didn't shave that much. Nobody would talk to him cause the whole thing was just too fuckin awful. But he didn't seem to mind and he wouldn't leave and he wouldn't disguise himself or somethin. He just stood there and stood there. Like a lighthouse.

MURK. Everybody knows this.

APRIL. Everybody forgets everything all the time, which is good maybe. But I remember. Until finally, everybody just got so demoralized by the sight a this bum priest standin there, that a buncha guys got together and chased him out. The posse. They ran Father Rogan outta town and into the arms a who knows what. Not me. So I didn't become a nun. I missed the logic there, but that's why I didn't go to India in black and white. Help me. Help me.

17

MURK. April.

APRIL. No. Help me. I've been in trouble for a long time, and it didn't make a fuck to me, but, my life's too long. I'm only thirty-two. I've got too much time to kill. I could live thirty, forty more years just starin at the meter runnin. I can't knock myself out enough. And too, I drink and things come outta me. The way I really am. The animal. The animal gets bigger all the time. She don't hardly fit in the fuckin haze no more. It's me and my animal. And I'm tryin to stay in and she's tryin to get out. That's when people go crazy.

MURK. April.

APRIL. No. When they can't stay the way they are no matter how they hit themselves in the head, and the teeth and the hair come rippin through everything dead that was walkin around. Like with the drinking. You drink and you drink. And the more you drink, the more it only goes through this one part of you, just this one part of you. And the more it goes through, the more it kills this part till that part's dead. So in the end or the middle I don't know where you're walkin around in this fuckin force field, you know, LIFE, and in there is this corpse and this animal fightin all the time, till the animal pushes off the dead weight and gets out, and that's when they take you away.

MURK. You gotta shut up.

APRIL. I don't wanna be the crazy one they take away.

SAVAGE. You gotta pull yourself together.

APRIL. Tell me somethin I don't know.

MURK. I'll take care of April.

SAVAGE. Sure you will. Give her another drink why don't you?

MURK. Get outta here if you're gonna talk that way.

SAVAGE. I got my drink here. I'm a payin customer. I'll talk till my mouth gets tired. April?

APRIL. What?

SAVAGE. We gotta get an apartment.

LINDA. Who?

SAVAGE. The me, you, the three of us.

LINDA. Oh, her now, too? You ain't serious now.

SAVAGE. Think about it. I'm scared and you're scared. But she's fuckin beyond. To help her we'll be able to do all the shit we're afraid a doin. We're no better off. But we can see her and

18

see there what we can't see in the mirror. When it's too hard to do straight out, we'll say we're doin it for her.

APRIL. That's nice.

LINDA. I don't wanna live with a woman like that.

SAVAGE. Wake up, Linda. We're a boxed set. Look at her. That's you. That's you.

LINDA. Alright. Let's find a place.

APRIL. Will I have my own room?

SAVAGE. Sure.

APRIL. That's nice, too. (*Tony Aronica has appeared in the audience aisle. He's a stream-lined Italian guy, open collar, thin gold chain at the neck, leather pants. He brings off the look very well, but he seems tentative, uncertain.*)

SAVAGE. Tony Aronica.

TONY. I know my name. (*He enters the stage.*)

LINDA. Anthony.

TONY. Hey, you think it was easy kissin off a fox like you? You don't know nothin.

SAVAGE. If you just blew in to run her down why don't you get lost?

TONY. Get outta my business. (*To Linda.*) You don't know nothin. That ain't right. That ain't what I meant. I gotta say what I mean. I feel like I'm just learnin to talk. It's hard. I saw somethin. That's why I tracked you down, Rotunda. What I said whadn't enough to say. You been nice. We had a nice little thing.

LINDA. Yeah, it was good.

TONY. I can smell the heat off you, you know that? The fire's never all the way out with you.

LINDA. Tony.

TONY. But that ain't what I came to say.

LINDA. What you want from me?

TONY. I was in my car outside this place over the weekend. I hadda a couple a drinks and I was a little fuzzy, so I was waitin till I cleared. It was dark. I was sittin there. And this unknown girl got in. She just got in the car. And she started talkin to me. She started rappin to me about the Soviet Union. Yeah. 'Bout their economy. Housin. How they feel about China bein right there. Everything. Everything about the Soviet Union. She musta

19

talked for two hours. Russian paranoia. Tass. The Gulag. I'm sittin there an I'm takin this in. The Trans-Siberian Railroad. What kinda tanks they got in Eastern Europe. Why they need American wheat. And then she was finished. She'd told me everything she knew. So I took her in the back seat and I banged her. And do you know something? It was the best. It was the best I ever had. And it whadn't cause she knew a lotta tricks or like that. It was cause she'd told me about the Soviet Union. And then she left. Now here's the thing. She was very ugly. I don't even wanna talk about how she looked. Mucho ugly. I didn't think I could ever be with a woman like that. But it came about outta whatever, happenstance, and I was. And it turned out to be better than what I went after. Do you see what I mean? Do you see what I'm comin towards? I always went for the girl like you. And what finally fuckin come to me, what finally fuckin penetrated the wall here, was there was somethin else. Somethin I never even thought about, didn't have a clue about. When I talked to you, I called it ugly girls. I don't know what to call it. There's other people. Like in science fiction. Another dimension right there but you can't see it. I got into it for a minute by accident. Through a crack. I caught a flash. The dimension a ugly girls. I'm like one a those guys inna factory and they bring in all new machines. That's what I feel like. Like I gotta retrain or I'm gonna lose my place. Some girls you look at some girls you don't. I wanna see the things I didn't see before an let the stuff I was lookin at go by. I've done the fuckin thing we're in, Linda. I've been with you, I talked to you. I know what that is. That's what I meant when I said you didn't know nothin, but I whadn't sayin it right. You look at what I look at. You know what I know. I wanna look at somethin else. I wanna know somethin else. I'm thirty-two years old. I wanna change.

LINDA. Now you're makin me mad.

TONY. I knew you wouldn't get it.

LINDA. I get it.

TONY. Like hell you do.

LINDA. What pisses me off is you think you know me. You don't know me.

TONY. Gimme a break, Linda. I know you like a book.

LINDA. You seen what I let you see, jerk. Nothin else. You

seen what I thought you could handle. What I thought you wanted to see. That's all. You don't know me.

TONY. What are you tellin me? You mean you knew about the Soviet Union?

LINDA. No, Einstein, that's not what I'm tellin you.

TONY. Then what?

LINDA. I feel like a ghost. I'm there and nobody sees me. I talk and nobody hears me.

APRIL. I hear you.

SAVAGE. Me too. Maybe they're the ghosts.

MURK. Boo.

TONY. Boo who? What the fuck are you, the abominable snowman? You know what's the matter with you people? All of you? You're not brave enough. That's right. Like in the old flicks when the guy stands up outta the ditch in the middle of the bombs blowin and flames and machine guns all over and just starts fightin back. Fuck it, right? You only live once. Is it gonna be on your knees? Stand up. You gotta be brave for yourself cause nobody else can be brave for you and nobody else cares. What the fuck, did you think you were gonna live forever? You're not. Stand up. It's pissin away. Your life. I know what I'm talkin about here so hear me good. Waste. It's like I wish they froze me inna block a ice till it was time and I was ready to make my move so I didn't waste anything. Waste, right? You clowns know about waste. I know about waste. I fuckin invented waste. I got this routine down with the girl the car and the bed, the girl the car and the bed, the girl the car and the bed, and I do it with this one part a my brain it's about this big, it's about the size of a piece of gum, and the rest of me I forgot to put away, right? I forgot to put it inna the refrigerator and it's startin to smell What's that smell? Oh, that's Tony Aronica. HE'S TURNIN FUCKIN GREEN.

LINDA. Well, smell Linda. Cause Linda's turnin fuckin green, too. I got news for you, chump. When you use this much a your brain on Linda, how much a Linda do you think you get? Huh? Figure it out. So that chick gave you the scoop on the Soviet Union. That's what the chick brought with her, shithead. What'd she leave with? What'd you give her? The same thing you gave me. A good bounce on the bed. Cause that's all you got in your

21

pocket to give. A good bounce. Ugly girls. Seriously, Anthony. You kill me.

TONY. You don't sound like yourself.

LINDA. Listen to you. I think you got about a five-watt bulb burnin in there. It's a miracle to me you can make your way around.

TONY. No, you are. You're talkin different.

LINDA. That's cause you're hittin me with a different level a stupidity than I'm used to. You sound like some mad doctor in some shitty movie. You're gonna steal ugly girl brains cause they don't got ugly girl brains on your planet.

SAVAGE. Lay off him.

LINDA. What?

SAVAGE. Don't you see the good thing? He's not thinkin like a dog. Do you know what it is for a guy like him to think with somethin asides his pecker? I didn't even think it was possible.

TONY. Hey, don't talk about me.

APRIL. I think you're cute. I'm not gonna do anything about it, but I think you're cute.

MURK. He's a type.

LINDA. Don't have too much to drink, April. You might get ugly. Then Tony'd be compulsed to put the make on you. And you're wrong, Savage. He is completely thinking with his pecker. His whole inspiration for this nutty fuckin idea was a good bounce in the back seat of his car and how he can get more of the same. (*To Tony.*) You're a moron. When you're not in bed, you're a moron.

APRIL. He doesn't look that stupid to me.

TONY. You don't wanna understand. I'm sorry I even tried to be straight with you. You're just as dumb as I thought you were. Just inna different way than I thought is all. You just want your Monday night workout, and then you don't wanna know from nothin. You probably wish I couldn't talk. You probably wish I was some kinda animal an ape a bull does what I do for you an then goes to sleep under a tree or some shit where I'm no bother. Well, that ain't me, the me I'm gonna be anyhow. You're a real cow, Linda. You're a real milker. An I'm not what's just good for some barnyard yahoo bullshit. No way. You're right. I don't know you. I thought you were a cow because you were a cow. Now I see you're a cow cause that's what you wanna be.

LINDA. Why don't you just fuckin die?

TONY. Cause I'm not in the mood, alright? I'm not in the mood to lay the fuck down an die.

LINDA. Well, what are you gonna do?

TONY. I'm gonna change.

LINDA. What?

TONY. From the ground. I'm gonna become a different person.

LINDA. You ain't got it in you.

TONY. I got tons in me.

SAVAGE. But how you get it out? Where you put it? Who's it for? You can't change. You can't do it. It's like puttin your hands on your own waist an tryin to pick yourself off the ground.

TONY. I am gonna do it, bitch. And you'd best not be in my way. I'm gonna go against my life with everything I got. I'm gonna attack my fuckin self as I am. I'm gonna kick ass and take names. And I am majorly majorly gonna change.

SAVAGE. What are you gonna change to?

TONY. I don't know. I'm gonna get new clothes. (*Indicating Murk.*) Maybe like his.

LINDA. What's wrong with your clothes?

TONY. They're mine.

LINDA. Changing clothes ain't gonna get you noplace.

TONY. You don't know that.

LINDA. You can change your clothes from now to New Year's, it ain't gonna do you dip. What you gotta do, Anthony sweetheart, is you gotta do your laundry. It ain't the new clothes that make the man. It's what he does with his dirty things. Do you hear what I'm sayin to you? You got yourself a shitload a laundry. You can walk away from that, but it'll still be there.

TONY. What are you talkin about? What laundry?

LINDA. Me, for instance.

SAVAGE. Linda. Why you pullin him back?

LINDA. Pullin him back from what? Where's he goin?

SAVAGE. I don't know. Outta some circle where he's been chokin. Hey, I got an idea. Maybe Tony could live with us, too.

TONY. Live with who?

SAVAGE. With me and April and Linda. We're gonna get a place, an apartment, an start a new life.

LINDA. And what exactly would be the arrangement, Denise?

SAVAGE. What d'you mean?

TONY. Three women?

LINDA. Don't even bother to get excited, Stud. (*To Savage.*) What the fuck you think this is, Manhattan?

SAVAGE. Don't be so quick, Linda. It's an idea. Think about it a minute.

LINDA. April, you, me, and him. In one apartment.

SAVAGE. Where do you live now, Tony?

TONY. In a garage. My uncle's gotta two-car garage and no car. So I keep my car in there, and a bed. A . . . I don't think I like this idea.

SAVAGE. Why not?

TONY. It sounds very nerve-wracking.

SAVAGE. So what?

TONY. It'd be like living in a fuckin hen house.

LINDA. I ain't doin it.

SAVAGE. Don't be so quick.

LINDA. My mother would swallow her tongue.

SAVAGE. Your mother wouldn't be livin with us.

LINDA. I won't share him.

TONY. I don't belong to you.

LINDA. Me more than them.

TONY. I don't belong to nobody.

LINDA. I won't share him.

SAVAGE. Alright. Alright then. You're out of it.

LINDA. What do you mean, I'm out of it?

SAVAGE. Tony, what I said before? About not bein able to change? I meant, not by yourself. I've thought about it a lot. It ain't possible.

LINDA. What do you mean, I'm out of it?

APRIL. Uh-oh.

SAVAGE. And you know it, too. That's why you're after some other kinda people to be with. I'm gonna tell you somethin, Tony. Somethin I can prove.

LINDA. Hey, Denise, what track you on?

APRIL. There are monkeys in this drink.

MURK. (*Instantly replacing her drink.*) No, there aren't.

SAVAGE. I never started the part of my life you always been in, Tony. And I've been readin books an thinkin an usin all the other parts a me you ain't been. I'm different than you.

TONY. You are?

24

SAVAGE. In every particle a me I'm different. Can't you feel it, Tony? Can't you feel the lack of chemistry between us?
TONY. I don't feel nothin.
SAVAGE. Exactly. I'm what you don't naturally want, so I am what you want if you want to change.
TONY. Whoa. I gotta think about that.
LINDA. Savage, what are you doin?
SAVAGE. I'm tryin to take him.
LINDA. What?
SAVAGE. You heard me. I'm tryin to take him away from you.
LINDA. You fuckin dirtbag.
SAVAGE. I told you I was waitin for somethin.
LINDA. You didn't say it was my boyfriend.
SAVAGE. You won't go along with me, Linda, I still gotta go.
APRIL. These monkeys have pitchforks and they're doin the LINDY.
SAVAGE. SNAP OUT OF IT, APRIL.
APRIL. I can't.
MURK. Leave her alone.
APRIL. Does this mean we're not gettin an apartment?
LINDA. Yeah, what about the apartment? You were gonna be my goddamn roommate girlfriend.
SAVAGE. I'm changin my plans.
LINDA. You never meant ta be my friend.
SAVAGE. Yes, I did, but it's gotta lead somewhere. If it's just another way not out then I gotta go for somethin else. Opportunity knocks like almost fuckin never. Tony.
LINDA. You are in physical danger, honey.
SAVAGE. I don't care.
LINDA. You will when you're missin a piece a your face.
SAVAGE. It's better than what I'm missing now. Tony, I'm a virgin.
TONY. What? What? Don't. Neither of you. This is interference. I don't know what I'm doin but I got my determination. You talk to me, it's like two bad angels pullin me down. Don't pull me down. I hadda friend Jimmy Rina, he blew up his sister with a nail bomb. So they locked him up for seven years. He got out last week. I saw him at a party. He was sittin inna chair. Some broad was ticklin his chin. But I could see. He was still in jail. They put you inna cage for seven years, the cage is in your

heart. No matter where you are. An I gotta cage in my heart, too. Solid steel this life has put in me. I'm lookin out through bars that come a knowin you an you an bein here an wearin these clothes an breathin this tired air. I want out. Don't make no sense. It's only my mind. What's that? Just a blob a bloody shit in my skull. I don't wanna be Tony Aronica no more. So neither a you got nothin ta say to me cause you don't even know who I am.

SAVAGE. You think you know who I am?

TONY. Oh, you too, huh? I don't care who you are, alright? I don't give a rusty fuck who you are. I got my own problems.

LINDA. I know who you are, darlin.

SAVAGE. Who?

LINDA. Another jive-ass man-grabbin broad who thinks every time she gets an ache it's another guy she needs.

SAVAGE. That's the worst description of me I ever heard.

LINDA. It'll do for now.

SAVAGE. But that's not how I am at all.

LINDA. I don't care. I don't gotta be fair with you. You're tryin ta grab my fuckin guy.

TONY. WOMEN.

LINDA. What's that supposed to mean?

TONY. I know. God fuckin forbid I should know something about women an say what it is. You got a hole in you. I didn't put it there. Remember that. It used to be such a goof playin with girls, too. Back on Archer Street. Back when you went to church or some fuckin place for what you come to me for now.

LINDA. You fuckin hypocrite motherfucker.

TONY. What?

LINDA. Did you or did you not sing me a fuckin song about ugly women who you are lookin to for a turnaround?

TONY. Yeah, but I'm not . . .

LINDA. So ain't you lookin to get from women just the same what I'm lookin to get from you?

TONY. Yeah maybe, but I'm . . .

LINDA. Then you're just a peg lookin for a hole same as the other way around is with me.

TONY. It's like I'm a ghost.

MURK. Oh, now you're a ghost, too.

TONY. That's right. Am I wrong? Don't nobody listen to no-

26

body except listenin for the trigger that sets them off on their thing. I mean when the fuck do we run out?

LINDA. Run outta what?

TONY. Run outta sayin . . . Run outta bein who I am.

LINDA. Never.

SAVAGE. Maybe very soon.

LINDA. Why you say shit outta the blue like that?

SAVAGE. We could run each other outta whatever, Tony, outta town?

TONY. My head hurts, man. I feel like my eyes are gonna cross.

MURK. HEY. (*To Tony.*) What are you drinkin?

TONY. Nothin.

MURK. Then get out.

SAVAGE. Hey, I'm talkin to him.

LINDA. No, I'm talkin to him.

MURK. Nobody stays in this bar without having a drink.

SAVAGE. He whadn't drinkin nothin before this.

MURK. That was the grace period.

SAVAGE. Then I'll buy him a drink. What are you drinkin?

TONY. I don't want nothin.

LINDA. Good.

SAVAGE. I'll buy him one anyway. Just put it on the bar.

LINDA. Don't you buy him no drink.

SAVAGE. I'll do what I damn well please.

LINDA. You put your hand in that bag, you're gonna get a fist in your face.

SAVAGE. You don't wanna do that, Linda.

LINDA. That's exactly what I want to do. Anybody buys Anthony a drink, it'll be me.

TONY. I don't want a drink.

LINDA. Who the fuck asked you? (*To Murk.*) Give him a Brandy Alexander.

APRIL. That's a beautiful drink.

TONY. I don't want it.

SAVAGE. He don't want your stupid Brandy Alexander.

APRIL. A really beautiful drink. A Christmas drink.

MURK. A Brandy Alexander is three dollars.

LINDA. I don't care if it's the jackpot in the Jersey lottery. Put the fuckin drink on the bar INSTANTLY. Here. (*Pays.*) You

27

know what I think? I think you can't trust the stars in the sky anymore. You can't trust anything anymore. (*Starts to cry.*)

MURK. Hey. Hey, don't cry.

APRIL. Murk hates cryin. It reminds him of his mother's tears over him.

SAVAGE. Hey Linda, I'm sorry. I didn't mean to . . . be the way I am.

TONY. She cries easy.

LINDA. (*Pauses from crying.*) You don't know me. (*Resumes.*)

TONY. Alright, I don't know you. You seem to cry easy. Hey, don't let it get to you, baby. Things ain't so bad.

SAVAGE. Yeah. Cheer up.

LINDA. Oh, I hate that.

SAVAGE. What?

LINDA. People tryin to cheer me up. Who asked you? I feel bad. I got a good reason to feel bad. Everybody's fuckin me over an lyin to me. My life eats it. I got no friends. I got nobody who loves me. My future looks like shit. I'm gettin fat. In ten years I'm gonna look like a rhino. You're tellin me to feel better. What are you, crazy? Get serious. I got nada to feel better about. What I got is a reason to cry. Don't try to take away what I got even if it stinks to give me nothin? My life sucks. Your life sucks. Your life sucks. Don't you tell me to stop cryin. You should start cryin. That's what should happen. You should all start cryin and banging your heads against the wall and permanently get off my fuckin case. Miserable buncha two-faced Doris Days.

TONY. Alright, so cry.

LINDA. (*Stops crying.*) Don't tell me what to do. (*Linda picks up the Brandy Alexander and drains it.*)

MURK. (*To Tony.*) This drink is empty. What are you drinking?

TONY. I don't want anything.

MURK. Then get out.

LINDA. (*To Murk.*) You should work for the city.

SAVAGE. Let me buy him one now. Don't make a big deal out of it. What are you drinkin?

TONY. Nothin.

LINDA. He's drinkin Brandy Alexanders.

APRIL. My mother drank four of those one Christmas, and she died.

28

SAVAGE. Alright, give him a Brandy Alexander.

APRIL. She drank four of 'em, and then she started breathin out. Ssss. And she never breathed in again. She exhaled and expired. (*April quietly sings "O Little Town Of Bethlehem" under the following.*)

MURK. Now I'm mad. You've upset April. She's gone Christmas. She always goes Christmas when she's upset. April. April. April.

SAVAGE. Hey. I'm a payin customer. Make the drink.

MURK. You can wait a minute. It's on order. Go to your table. (*Murk puts on little rectangular glasses and applies red rouge to his cheeks.*)

TONY. What's he doin?

LINDA. I don't know.

SAVAGE. Murk? (*Murk dons a white beard, and puts on the jacket and hat of a Santa suit.*)

MURK. The problem with people is they think they're alone. They think what they say don't do nothin. So they say every stupid thing that goes through their gourd, and they do shit they don't even know why. Which leads to what? The world looks like homemade refried shit. Jingle bells jingle bells, jingle all the way . . .

APRIL. Is that you, Santa?

MURK. Ho ho ho. It's me, April.

APRIL. It's good to see you.

MURK. It's good to see you, too, April.

APRIL. Did you get my letter?

MURK. Yes.

APRIL. I didn't know how to address it.

MURK. I got it.

APRIL. I thought you might pass me right by. I've been bad.

MURK. I forgive you.

APRIL. You do?

MURK. Yes.

APRIL. Really?

MURK. Yes. I've brought you something.

APRIL. You have?

MURK. (*Taking a nicely wrapped Christmas present from a refrigerator underneath the bar.*) A present. I brought it all the way from the North Pole.

APRIL. I don't deserve a present.

MURK. Yes, you do. You're a good girl, April.

APRIL. Am I?

MURK. You're a good girl in a good world. And because you are, my helpers and I worked very hard and made you this. The box may feel a little cold. I just brought it from the North Pole.

APRIL. Thank you. It does feel cold. (*She unwraps the present. It's a music box. She opens it. It plays.*)

MURK. Merry Christmas, April.

APRIL. Merry Christmas.

MURK. Do you like it?

APRIL. More than anything.

MURK. Now promise me you'll be a good girl.

APRIL. I promise.

MURK. And you'll say your prayers?

APRIL. Yes.

MURK. And you won't go crazy?

APRIL. No.

MURK. Alright then. (*Takes music box and puts it away.*) Jingle bells jingle bells, jingle all the way . . . (*To himself, as he gets out of the Santa attire.*) Everybody's doin it to everybody, and everybody's saying they don't know why it's happening. It's happening because they're doin it. It's a matter a cause and effect. It's a matter a responsibility. People gotta take responsibility for what they do. (*To Savage.*) Now, that was a Brandy Alexander, right?

SAVAGE. Right.

APRIL. Hey Murk, top me off a little, okay? I'm losin my head.

MURK. I'll be with you inna minute, April.

APRIL. Okay.

TONY. What did I just see?

MURK. Don't make a big thing out of it.

TONY. But what was that? You were bein Santa Claus.

MURK. Don't make a big thing, I said.

APRIL. Murk don't like that. When you talk about how he is.

MURK. It's no good. You can kill a thing like that.

LINDA. You were nice to her.

MURK. Talk about somethin else.

SAVAGE. You made like you were Saint Nick. You got the clothes an everything.

MURK. TONY. Do something for once in your life. Talk about somethin else.

TONY. What?

MURK. I don't care. Somethin that don't have me in it.

TONY. Okay. I can't think a nothin.

LINDA. This does not surprise me.

SAVAGE. That's why you need me, Tony. Cause you don't know nothin but the girl the car and the bed.

TONY. And the Soviet Union.

SAVAGE. Oh yeah? Talk to me about the Soviet Union.

TONY. They need our wheat.

SAVAGE. Why?

TONY. I can't.

SAVAGE. Why not?

TONY. I'm forgettin what it was.

SAVAGE. You know why? Cause it was never yours. The ugly girl brought you somethin and then she took it away. You never had it to keep. Now I see my mistake. If I offer you my virginity and you take it, you're right back where you were. And that's where you'd take me, too.

TONY. Hey look, I didn't ask you to figure out my whole . . .

SAVAGE. If I offer you my virginity, and you take it, then that'd really just be me takin Linda's place.

LINDA. Who'd want my place?

SAVAGE. Right. We'd just be ruttin in the same rut you was ruttin in before.

TONY. I don't get it you.

SAVAGE. That's right. You don't. I went another way. I'm sealed up like a jug a wine's been layin in the ocean since the Romans. I'm a find. You want me, Tony, I'm found.

TONY. Maybe. Maybe there is somethin in you for me.

SAVAGE. Maybe.

LINDA. Ain't I got things in me same as her?

SAVAGE. You're a pig. You gave it away. You just gave it away.

LINDA. (*Makes for Savage; stops.*) I don't wanna kill. I wanna win. I spare you.

SAVAGE. This is my offer. My virginity. It's a place. On the map if you know what I mean. You can't go there cause a where

31

you been but I am there and I can take you there. You say you wanna break outta this prison life that's got you tied up in some cage but you don't know how. Here's how. Live with me. Inna room. With no bed.

TONY. With no bed. With no bed? Meaning no . . . (*Gestures.*)

SAVAGE. That's right.

TONY. That's a new one. That's a brand new wrinkle. It's got about as much appeal for me as cancer, but it's new. You know, I'm depressed. I'm fucked up and depressed.

LINDA. Tony, you were right. I was a cow for you. But I don't have to be no cow. It's cause I thought that's what you wanted. A good bounce and goodbye, right? So I was wrong. Shoot me. But I wasn't wrong, was I? It was what you wanted till lately, ain't it? So now you're changin. So? Can't I change, too? Don't you see how I wanna change? Can it make any fuckin sense in any way to keep startin from zero every time it's time to make a move? Take me with you. Anthony, we'll go somewhere. Do you really wanna live your whole life leavin people, tryin ta keep up with yourself? Ain't you afraid a gettin lonely? Ain't you? It can be all there is, baby. Think your thoughts and get outrageous, but just remember, you could end up alone. It's how a lotta people end up. Look around. I don't haveta tell you nothin. Open your eyes it's there to see. Like dead leaves floatin in the water. (*To Savage.*) So you're a virgin. The only thing you never used was your body. But up there. In there's your tired old pig brain ain't been off its back since the Flood. Probably reeks in there like dirty sheets an last month's rag. What's so sweet about that? I'm hungry. I wanna bite somethin. (*Takes the newly made drink and downs it.*) Very tasty.

APRIL. That's two she's had. Two more an she's gone.

TONY. I'm leavin. (*Tony exits into the audience.*)

SAVAGE. Where you goin?

TONY. I don't know.

LINDA. You goin back to your place?

SAVAGE. Stay. (*Tony is in the audience aisle. He turns and faces the stage.*)

TONY. What? In a room with no bed? With you? Doin what?

LINDA. I gotta suggestion. Marry me.

TONY. What?

APRIL. Oh my God. A proposal.

LINDA. Marry me.

SAVAGE. What's this?

LINDA. Action.

SAVAGE. That's not what I meant.

LINDA. I don't care what you meant. You wanna marry me, Tony? You wanna marry me, we could get married. You want different? It'd be different. It'd be a trip.

SAVAGE. That is so tired. That is so old.

LINDA. Ain't nobody in this room's ever done it.

SAVAGE. That don't make it new.

LINDA. I ain't tryin to be original.

SAVAGE. Maybe that's your problem.

LINDA. And maybe your problem is you're tryin to invent the wheel.

SAVAGE. I'M TRYIN. What am I tryin? To rise up. People who died a minute an came back, they say they saw . . . They rose up outta an saw themselves. An what a relief. What am I tryin? I had this dream. It haunts me. It fuckin haunts me. I was lookin inna mirror. An I noticed a bit of the skin on my cheek was peelin so I pulled it off. Then I saw a bigger piece was peelin an I pulled that off, too. An inna few minutes I'd pulled off my whole face like it was tissues. An I looked in the mirror, and all that was there was a piece of flat grey cardboard where my face had been. An I was glad. I was glad my face was gone. An somebody said to me, God, you've got beautiful eyes. An that was what was left I saw. Just my eyes and the rest blank. An I said, they were always there an they were always beautiful, but now you can really see them cause there's nothing else. I'm not gonna ask you to marry me, Tony. Linda is offerin one thing and I am offerin you somethin else. I'm tryin to pull off my face so you can see my eyes. Do you wanna see my eyes?

TONY. What the fuck are you talkin about? I feel like they're offerin me some choice from the moon. This one says I gotta do my laundry, an this one's gonna rip off her face.

LINDA. Who do you want, me or her?

TONY. I don't know what to say to you.

LINDA. She's a virgin. She's thirty-two and she's a virgin. That's just sad if you know what I mean. She ain't never done

33

no lovin and now she's startin to get desperate. Is that what you need? Some desperate broad ain't gonna save you from nothin.

SAVAGE. I hate you.

LINDA. I can live with that.

SAVAGE. You hit me where it's easiest.

LINDA. That's where it makes sense to hit.

APRIL. I got somethin to say.

MURK. April.

APRIL. Tony, will you marry me?

TONY. Are you talkin to me?

APRIL. Why don't you marry me? I don't take up much room.

MURK. Well Tony, are you gonna marry her?

TONY. No.

MURK. Good.

APRIL. I'm a little disappointed, Tony. I thought we mighta hadda real future.

SAVAGE. Oh man, the future. Is the future really in these fuckin old cards?

LINDA. Fuck the future. Tony, you walk outta here without me where you goin? You're not takin a step. You're nowhere. I'm nowhere. I'm bein serious with you, Aronica.

TONY. Man, this is hard. I didn't know things was this hard.

SAVAGE. You coulda stayed asleep till you were dead. What's worse? Tony, I do believe there is another kinda livin that don't have deadness in it. I'm offerin you somethin here, somethin unknown, somethin yet to come. Somethin the smartness hasn't gotten at with its names. (*Tony steps back on stage.*)

TONY. (*Gently.*) What are you doin?

SAVAGE. I'm tryin to start somethin . . . new.

TONY. It don't work.

LINDA. I'll show you what works. (*Linda goes to Tony, kisses him. They get very hot together. Then she stops, turns him around and turns around herself, so they're back to back. She puts her arms through his arms, and picks him up off the ground, stretching him. Then she throws him off, and steps away.*)

TONY. That was definitely good.

APRIL. I'm a little jealous.

LINDA. Ain't nobody gonna make it happen for you like me.

MURK. April?

APRIL. What?

MURK. Will you marry me?

APRIL. I think I'm losin my head, Murk.

MURK. I'll marry you if you promise that we'll go on just exactly like now. No changes of any kind.

SAVAGE. Then why would you wanna get married at all?

MURK. To keep things the same. I'm thirty-two years old. Well?

APRIL. Well . . . No.

MURK. Oh.

APRIL. I like bein foot loose an fancy free.

MURK. Uh-huh.

APRIL. I like havin my options open.

MURK. Uh-huh.

APRIL. I like it that if we got somethin goin it's cause we choose to have somethin goin, an it's not outta feelin we should or somethin weird like that. Do you understand what I mean?

MURK. Yeah. You're cut off. No more credit, no more drinks.

APRIL. I accept your proposal.

MURK. Thank you. You've made me a happy man.

LINDA. If you're so happy, why don't you go on an crack a smile?

MURK. No, I don't think I'll do that. April, I'll buy you a drink. Since you're my intended.

APRIL. I'll have a Brandy Alexander, in one of the large glasses, served on a white doily.

MURK. Alright.

APRIL. As I have told you all, this is the very drink that killed my mother. My father died of nothin at all, which is maybe the saddest thing a person can pass on from. But my mother, who was the only one ever stupid enough to love me, my mother died from this drink that Murk is making me now. I have always taken consolation where I could find it, even when it caused me grief.

MURK. (*Serving the drink on the doily.*) Here.

LINDA. You know, I put the fuckin question to you, Anthony, an you got me hangin.

SAVAGE. Me too.

LINDA. I can't even take you seriously, Denise. With you it's just an idea in your mind. An not a very clear idea. With me, it's my life.

SAVAGE. Don't you think it's my life, too? Cause it is.

35

LINDA. Then your life is just an unclear idea in your mind cause you ain't livin that I can see. What are you waitin for, anyway? Bein a virgin at your age. Get serious. What kinda silly shit is that? I've had three kids. One of 'em my aunt took. The other two went to nobody I know. Which broke my heart. But I've had three kids. An I didn't hang no shit on nobody when I got in the family way because this is my life, understand? This is my life, my circus, my boat to row. I'll do what I do an take what comes. One a those kids was yours.

TONY. WHAT?

LINDA. That's right, Mr. Wizard. About time you knew. An did I come to you? I take my shit alone. You've got a son. He lives with my aunt. His name is Alphonse.

APRIL. Congratulations.

TONY. Shut up.

APRIL. Sorry.

LINDA. What? You as bad as her? You been dreamin your life'd start when you said go? It's on, man. The movie has been on for a while. An look what you been missin outta your stupidity. You missed the birth of your own son. But you see now I'm tired. I've carried so many boys. (*To Savage.*) What have you carried? Some lock on your heart. Runnin around yellin in your stainless steel panties.

SAVAGE. Don't.

LINDA. I don't mean to be mean. But you come against me, I gotta hold my own. (*To Tony.*) An I'll tell you somethin else, Lancelot. I am currently in the family way with another Aronica offspring.

TONY. You ain't serious now.

LINDA. I gotta laugh at you. You gotta forgive me. But you ain't got a clue. You ain't flipped the knob on your box inna long time, have you? There are people out here, chum. There are other stories than the one you're in. You're so sure you're the sun, an the moon an the stars spin around you, an God made you an the rest of us is just decoration, right? Like if the flood comes, you'll be Noah, huh? I do doubt it. Not that that's an issue with me. I could care less.

TONY. What's the kid look like?

LINDA. He's fuckin repulsive, alright?

TONY. Okay, I deserved that.

MURK. This drink is empty. Tony, what are you drinking?

SAVAGE. Oh, would you get off that kick?

MURK. You have to have a drink you're drinking. If you're finished, you leave.

SAVAGE. Who made up that rule?

MURK. I did.

SAVAGE. Well, the drink's been empty for twenty minutes. Why you enforcin it now?

MURK. It's not empty till I say it's empty.

SAVAGE. Why'd you dress up like Santa Claus?

MURK. Shut up, Savage.

SAVAGE. I feel like I can never get past the goddamn thing here. There's the thing, and then there's what you think about it. But around here, there's just the thing.

LINDA. You talk for everybody. Maybe you should just talk for yourself.

MURK. (*To Tony.*) This drink is empty. What are you drinking?

SAVAGE. You can't just keep fillin 'em up an we empty 'em and the night goes by and it's the next day and it's the same thing. That's death. That's death. We gotta get past the thing. We gotta break the sameness. Murk?

MURK. I don't see that. You think a bomb in the works is better than going on the same?

SAVAGE. I believe in action.

MURK. You wanna run around till you're tired, go for it. Knock yourself out. (*To Tony.*) This drink is empty. What are you drinking?

SAVAGE. He's not drinking nothin. How can you keep it up? What's the fuckin point? I mean if this is all you're gonna do for the rest of your life and you know it, why bother to play it out? If you seen the fuckin cards an the future's there an the future's this an nothin more, like a book where every page's the same, why not drop a rock on yourself an die? If every time a glass is empty you're gonna say What are you drinkin, no matter how you feel no matter who it is, then you could be anybody nobody, a machine jerkin when you smack the button, a wall kids bounce balls off, the rope I hang myself with. What's the point? What's the point? (*To Tony.*) What was my crime that I got life?

TONY. Anyone knows the answer to that one, it'd be you. I don't know how to be in your shoes. I don't even know how to

37

be in mine. I don't even wanna be in mine. But here I am. The shoe fits an I'm wearin it. And there's a lot that goes with that. Live with that a minute. I have to.

MURK. This drink is empty. What are you drinking?

TONY. Nothin. And you live with that a minute. I have a son?

LINDA. Yup.

TONY. His name's Alphonse?

LINDA. Yup.

TONY. Who named him that?

LINDA. Me.

TONY. And does it like, stick?

LINDA. Yeah, it sticks. It's his name.

TONY. Why didn't you tell me?

LINDA. Don't make me laugh, alright?

TONY. Alright. Alright.

LINDA. Alright what?

TONY. I'm thinkin. Alright.

LINDA. Alright what?

TONY. Would you be cool a minute? Where's the baby?

LINDA. My aunt's got it.

TONY. Can you get it back?

LINDA. Yeah, maybe.

MURK. Get out, Tony.

TONY. YOU KNOW THESE PLANTS ARE DEAD. You oughta throw them out.

MURK. Those plants are very reliable.

TONY. Linda, I don't know you.

LINDA. I know you don't. But you know me.

TONY. I wanna do like eight different things.

LINDA. Then but do what you want.

TONY. You say yes to one thing, you say no to a lotta the others causa the yes.

LINDA. If ya don't make up your mind ta somethin, you'll go bad.

SAVAGE. That's not what action is.

LINDA. You know, you're the leadin authority on nothin. I've just about had it with you. You ain't taken a step since I known ya. Why don't you have a couple a drinks an go out an fuck somebody? (*A big pause.*)

TONY. I'll take a Brandy Alexander.

MURK. Alright.

APRIL. I think the thing you don't appreciate, Denise, is routine.

SAVAGE. You know what I think?

APRIL. What?

SAVAGE. I think you should go off your nut.

MURK. Hey.

SAVAGE. Why don't you just go ahead an fuckin lose it?

APRIL. You really don't know what you're sayin.

SAVAGE. You put yourself in the nuthouse, babe. That's what I think. You put on a fresh straightjacket every mornin before you take your first twitch.

MURK. Lay off her.

SAVAGE. Like there's somebody on April's case. There's never anybody on April's case.

MURK. I'm serious, Savage. Shut up.

SAVAGE. And you're the gatekeeper around here, ain't you? You're the one keeps the spooks in the cemetery.

LINDA. You know, you're crazy. You're all over the place.

SAVAGE. You think so?

LINDA. Yeah, I do. I come in here cryin, you tell me we should be friends an getta apartment. And April, too. Then my boyfriend comes in and you start hittin on him, and forget me, right? Now you tell April she should go crazy. Which is a bad idea. How am I supposed to think about you, Denise?

SAVAGE. I don't care. I don't care how you think about me. What d'you want? You want me to act like somebody on T.V.? This one got this one way an that's how they are? I don't know how I am, who I am. I don't know what I believe. I don't know where to go to find out. I don't know what to do to be the one person that somewhere inside I wanna be. I don't know nothin but the one thing: I gotta move. And you, too. This whole world I'm in's gotta break up an move.

MURK. Get out.

SAVAGE. I gotta drink in fronta me I ain't finished. We're on the cliff. We were born here. Well, do you wanna die on the cliff? Do you wanna die in bed? Do you think you're gonna live forever? They told us if you jump off the cliff, you die. And you probably do, but fuck it. Fuck it. We don't know that. You don't know nothin you ain't done, an nobody can tell you nothin. Ain't you tired a livin if this is all livin is? And you know it's not. I may be an asshole and I may not know what to do, but you hear what I'm sayin to you, dammit you do. In your heart you do. This is not life. This is not life. This is not life. Ugly women, right Tony? Somethin else. I don't care what. God, gimme somethin else cause this is definitely not it. New eyes new ears new hands. Gimme back my soul from where you took it, gimme back my friends, gimme back my priests an my father, and take this goddamn virginity from off my life. HUNGER HUNGER HUNGER. If somebody don't gimme somethin, I'm gonna die. I wanna play pool. (*Picks up the pool cue and uses it as a spear or a wand.*) Somebody play pool with me. (*No one moves.*) I come in here a lotta nights, a lotta nights, an I play pool by myself. I like the game. You hit the white ball, and that ball hits another, and it goes somewhere. When I first started, I didn't mind playin alone. But you get tired of it. The balls don't do nothin unless you make 'em do it. It's all you. They're just like stones. It's like I'm some woman lives inna cave and plays with stones. Somebody play pool with me. You be the cue ball. Hit me and I'll fly. You don't wanna jump yourself, push me off. You can't keep up your courage alone, playin with stones.

MURK. What d'you want, Savage?

SAVAGE. I don't want you inna red suit, takin me back where I can't go.

TONY. Come on. You want me to play pool with you, I'll play pool with you.

SAVAGE. No.

APRIL. You want me to be a nun and go to India?

SAVAGE. No.

LINDA. Do you wanna be friends?

SAVAGE. I don't know how.

LINDA. Alright. Goodbye. (*To Tony.*) Will you marry me or what?

TONY. Hey, gimme room.

LINDA. I gave you room, but I didn't hear nothin comin forth.

TONY. Well, gimme room now. I feel like I'm under the gun here. But maybe, I don't know, maybe that's the way things really are. Alright. We'll get a place.

LINDA. A place?

TONY. Yeah, a place.

LINDA. Will we be married in this place?

TONY. Absofuckinlutely not.

LINDA. Why not?

TONY. Because your wish is not my command, Rotunda. You wanna live with me or not?

LINDA. I wanna get married.

TONY. I know that. But that is not what I wanna do, so I ain't gonna do that. But I do wanna do somethin. Do you wanna do somethin to change our situation or what? Do you wanna live with me?

LINDA. Yeah. I wanna move outta my whole house. I wanna live with you.

TONY. Then we'll get a place an we'll live together seven days the week. You wanna claim that kid or what?

LINDA. Yeah, I want the kid.

TONY. Alphonse.

LINDA. Alphonse Aronica.

SAVAGE. Linda?

LINDA. Yeah?

SAVAGE. Goodbye.

APRIL. (*To Savage.*) You want me to do somethin?

MURK. April?

APRIL. Yeah?

MURK. We're gettin married.

APRIL. Right.

SAVAGE. You said there was an animal.

APRIL. Yes.

SAVAGE. There is. There is. There's one in me, too. Big scary fuckin animal. It's the only thing in me that I love. It wasn't always. It's just that these days, these days, it's the only thing in me, it's the only thing in everybody, that ain't a total fuckin horrible lie. I. AM. ALONE.

MURK. Closing time. Last call. Last call. Last call. (*Blackout.*)

THE END

PROPERTY LIST

ONSTAGE

Dead plants (2)
Small rectangular tables (2)
Chairs (2)
Stool
Glasses
Watering can
Rectangular eyeglasses
Red rouge
White beard
Jacket and hat of Santa suit
Christmas present
Refrigerator
Music box
Pool cue

OFFSTAGE

Black bag (Savage)
Pack of cards (worn) (Savage)
Money

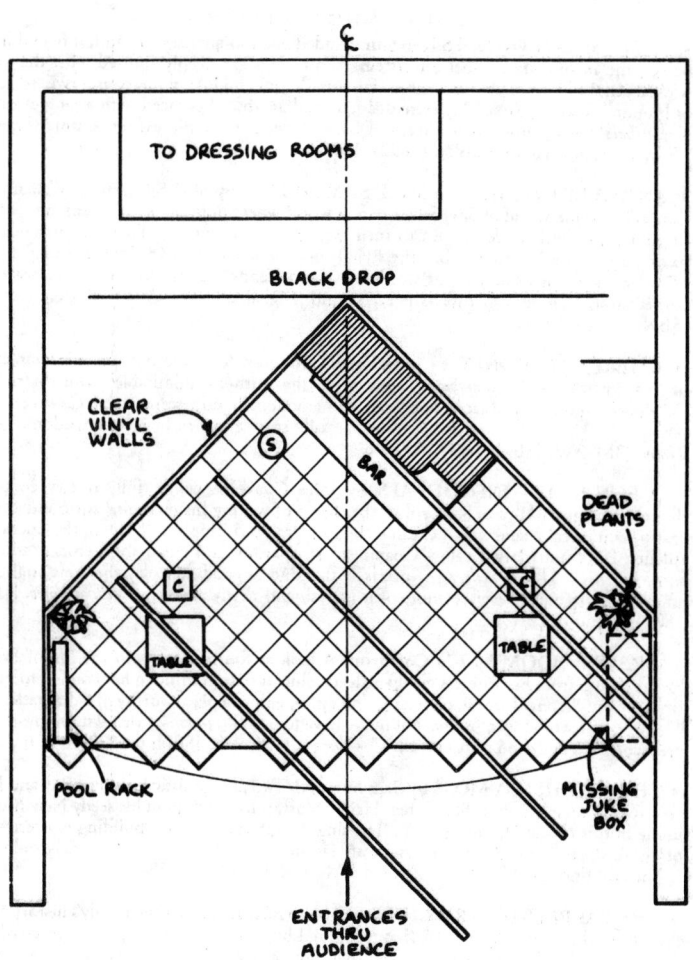

TO DRESSING ROOMS

BLACK DROP

CLEAR VINYL WALLS

Ⓢ

BAR

DEAD PLANTS

Ⓒ

TABLE

Ⓒ

TABLE

POOL RACK

MISSING JUKE BOX

ENTRANCES THRU AUDIENCE

SCENE DESIGN
"SAVAGE IN LIMBO"

43

NEW PLAYS

★ **SHEL'S SHORTS by Shel Silverstein.** Lauded poet, songwriter and author of children's books, the incomparable Shel Silverstein's short plays are deeply infused with the same wicked sense of humor that made him famous. "...[a] childlike honesty and twisted sense of humor." –*Boston Herald*. "...terse dialogue and an absurdity laced with a tang of dread give [*Shel's Shorts*] more than a trace of Samuel Beckett's comic existentialism." –*Boston Phoenix*. [flexible casting] ISBN: 0-8222-1897-6

★ **AN ADULT EVENING OF SHEL SILVERSTEIN by Shel Silverstein.** Welcome to the darkly comic world of Shel Silverstein, a world where nothing is as it seems and where the most innocent conversation can turn menacing in an instant. These ten imaginative plays vary widely in content, but the style is unmistakable. "...[*An Adult Evening*] shows off Silverstein's virtuosic gift for wordplay...[and] sends the audience out...with a clear appreciation of human nature as perverse and laughable." –*NY Times*. [flexible casting] ISBN: 0-8222-1873-9

★ **WHERE'S MY MONEY? by John Patrick Shanley.** A caustic and sardonic vivisection of the institution of marriage, laced with the author's inimitable razor-sharp wit. "...Shanley's gift for acid-laced one-liners and emotionally tumescent exchanges is certainly potent..." –*Variety*. "...lively, smart, occasionally scary and rich in reverse wisdom." –*NY Times*. [3M, 3W] ISBN: 0-8222-1865-8

★ **A FEW STOUT INDIVIDUALS by John Guare.** A wonderfully screwy comedy-drama that figures Ulysses S. Grant in the throes of writing his memoirs, surrounded by a cast of fantastical characters, including the Emperor and Empress of Japan, the opera star Adelina Patti and Mark Twain. "Guare's smarts, passion and creativity skyrocket to awesome heights..." –*Star Ledger*. "...precisely the kind of good new play that you might call an everyday miracle...every minute of it is fresh and newly alive..." –*Village Voice*. [10M, 3W] ISBN: 0-8222-1907-7

★ **BREATH, BOOM by Kia Corthron.** A look at fourteen years in the life of Prix, a Bronx native, from her ruthless girl-gang leadership at sixteen through her coming to maturity at thirty. "...vivid world, believable and eye-opening, a place worthy of a dramatic visit, where no one would want to live but many have to." –*NY Times*. "...rich with humor, terse vernacular strength and gritty detail..." –*Variety*. [1M, 9W] ISBN: 0-8222-1849-6

★ **THE LATE HENRY MOSS by Sam Shepard.** Two antagonistic brothers, Ray and Earl, are brought together after their father, Henry Moss, is found dead in his seedy New Mexico home in this classic Shepard tale. "...His singular gift has been for building mysteries out of the ordinary ingredients of American family life..." –*NY Times*. "...rich moments ...Shepard finds gold." –*LA Times*. [7M, 1W] ISBN: 0-8222-1858-5

★ **THE CARPETBAGGER'S CHILDREN by Horton Foote.** One family's history spanning from the Civil War to WWII is recounted by three sisters in evocative, intertwining monologues. "...bittersweet music—[a] rhapsody of ambivalence...in its modest, garrulous way...theatrically daring." –*The New Yorker*. [3W] ISBN: 0-8222-1843-7

★ **THE NINA VARIATIONS by Steven Dietz.** In this funny, fierce and heartbreaking homage to *The Seagull*, Dietz puts Chekhov's star-crossed lovers in a room and doesn't let them out. "A perfect little jewel of a play..." –*Shepherdstown Chronicle*. "...a delightful revelation of a writer at play; and also an odd, haunting, moving theater piece of lingering beauty." –*Eastside Journal (Seattle)*. [1M, 1W (flexible casting)] ISBN: 0-8222-1891-7

DRAMATISTS PLAY SERVICE, INC.
440 Park Avenue South, New York, NY 10016 212-683-8960 Fax 212-213-1539
postmaster@dramatists.com www.dramatists.com